THE CURSE OF
ST. TRINIAN'S

Founder's Day

Ronald Searle

The Curse of St. Trinian's

THE BEST OF THE DRAWINGS

PAVILION

This anthology has been selected from drawings
originally published under the following titles:

Hurrah for St. Trinian's!, London 1948
The Female Approach, London 1949
Back to the Slaughterhouse, London 1951
The Terror of St. Trinian's, London 1952
Souls in Torment, London 1953
The Female Approach, New York 1954
Merry England, etc., London 1956
The St. Trinian's Story, London 1959

This selection first published in Great Britain in 1993 by
PAVILION BOOKS LIMITED
196 Shaftesbury Avenue, London WC2H 8JL

Artwork production by Bet Ayer

A CIP catalogue record for this book
is available from the British Library.

ISBN 1 85793 0711

Printed and bound in Great Britain by Butler & Tanner Ltd

10 9 8 7 6 5 4 3 2 1

This book may be ordered by post direct from the publisher.
Please contact the Marketing Department. But try your bookshop first.

A Word from Our Sponsor

At last! After almost half a century on the run, the St. Trinian's drawings finally have a book to themselves. For the benefit of those who identify the belles of St. Trinian's with black-and-white films from the Fifties starring Alastair Sim in drag that turn up with masochistic regularity as British Comedy Classics on TV, here are the roots. This is where it all came from.

I was barely out of my teens when the idea was conceived and many shrill voices said that the baby should have been aborted. Apart from a first isolated drawing published in *Lilliput* magazine in 1941, made as a private joke for two schoolgirl sisters attending St. Trinnean's school for young ladies in Edinburgh, the cartoons ran for a mere seven years from 1946, until I killed them off in my book: *Souls in Torment* in 1953. But they refused to lie down.

In addition to my sister, another ex-Cambridge schoolgirl, P.D. James, is possibly one of the first models for the girls, and seeing what has emerged from *her* head since she left school, it is not surprising that St. Trinian's took on the flavour it did – transforming the public image of schoolgirls by dragging them out of the nineteenth century.

Since those days reality has more than overtaken fantasy and, in the light of some of the adolescent *fin de siècle* activity today, my original reputation as a father of *humour noir* has paled into *humour rose*.

However, I am not going to get myself involved further in that discussion, having just signed another St. Trinian's film contract...

R.S., 1992

Our Philosophy
(For those who came in late)

Maidens of St. Trinian's
Gird your armour on.
Grab the nearest weapon
Never mind which one!
The battle's to the strongest
Might is always right.
Trample on the weakest
Glory in their plight!
St. Trinian's! St. Trinian's!
Our battle cry.
St. Trinian's! St. Trinian's!
Will never die!
Stride towards your fortune,
Boldly on your way.
Never once forgetting
There's one born every day.
Let our motto be broadcast
'Get your blow in first',
She who draws the sword last
Always comes off worst.

Sidney Gilliat [1954]

[1941]

'Owing to the international situation the match
with St. Trinian's has been postponed.'

'Hand up the girl who burnt down the East Wing last night.'

'Well, that's O.K. – now for old "Stinks".'

'Oh my God, she's put water with it again.'

'Bang goes another pair of knuckledusters.'

'Prudence is new to St. Trinian's,
  I want you to take care of her, girls.'

'But I only broke her leg, Miss.'

'Go on, say it – "I promise to leave my body to Science".'

'Hell! My best scotch.'

'I must not smoke Pot during prayers.
I must not smoke Pot during...'

'Fair play, St. Trinian's, use a clean needle.'

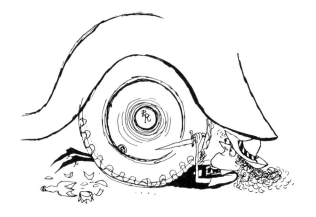

'Little Maisy's our problem child.'

'We'd better have her examined, she's resolved to be good.'

'All right! All right! I'll join the union.'

'Oh my God, she's in love.'

'A dozen of that one, please.'

'Well, you said your love knew no bounds.'

'O.K. Make it a Krug rosé and a packet of nuts.'

SCHOOL HOLS

'Life will be just a hollow mockery without you, Drusilla.'

'But, Miss Merryweather, you *said* we could bring our pets back with us.'

'Come along, prefects. Playtime over.'

'Girls, girls! – a little less noise, please.'

'I'll just die and then you'll be sorry.'

'She's just discovered that Rambo is married.'

'Could you tell me the time, please?'

'... of course indoor games are an extra.'

'Playing with lethal weapons, a boy of your age...'

'Cynthia! How many times must I tell you to
take the band off *before* you light up...'

'O.K. – pass the bat's blood.'

'Who's there?'

'And please rain fire and brimstone on the lot.'

'Now ask him to abolish homework.'

'Honestly, darling, you don't look a day over nine.'

'Eunice, dear, aren't we rather muddling our patron saints?'

'It's WINE!'

'And this is Rachel, our head girl.'

'Cleaners getting slack, Horsefall.'

'Well done, Cynthia, it WAS Deadly Nightshade.'

'Look, Miss, the spirit of Botany.'

'Dump those, they're harmless.'

'Some little girl didn't hear me say "unarmed combat".'

'Why can't he let down his hair, or something?'

'Well actually, Miss Tonks, my soul *is* in torment.'

'Ruddy music lessons...'

'Shitty Stockhausen!'

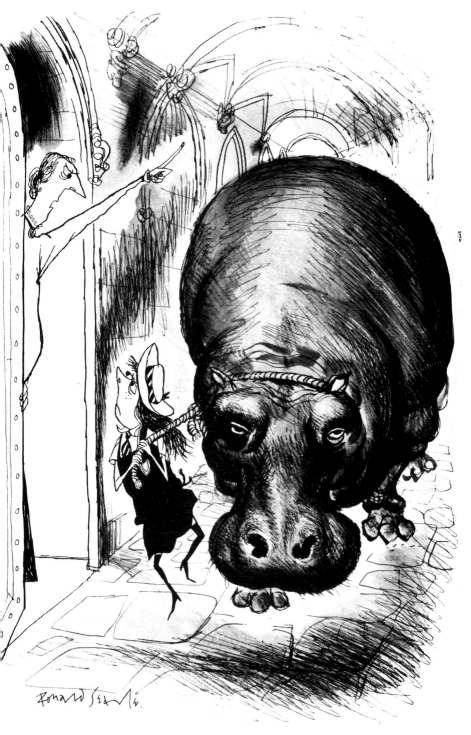

'Elspeth! Put that back AT ONCE.'

'Bloody sportsdays...'

'I didn't realise it took so long.'

A Short Dirge for St. Trinian's

Where are the girls of yesteryear? How strange
To think they're scattered East, South, West and North –
Those pale Medusas of the Upper Fourth,
Those Marihuanas of the Moated Grange.

No more the shrieks of victims, and no more
The fiendish chuckle borne along the breeze!
Gone are the basilisk eyes, the bony knees.
Mice, and not blood, run down each corridor.

Now poison ivy twines the dorm where casks
Were broached and music mistresses were flayed,
While on the sports ground where the pupils played
The relatively harmless adder basks.

Toll for St. Trinian's, nurse of frightful girls!
St. Trinian's, mother of the far too free!
No age to come (thank God) will ever see
Such an academy as Dr. Searle's.

C. Day Lewis [1953]

'Cynthia, you really *are* The End.'